# *Praise for the First Edition*
## Home Sweet Home Page

"Carma's book on creating Web sites in the era of Web 2.0 is the simplest, most readable, and best in a highly cluttered market."

**— Elatia Harris, Founder, Tessa's Table 2050**

"Even though she is an accomplished website and graphic design professional AND Internet marketer, Carma speaks in plain English and keeps things simple. And she still includes pretty much everything I would want you to know about building an effective online presence—and how to do it right from the start!"

**— Linda Dessau, Founder, You Talk, I'll Write**

"The power of the book is how Carma Spence packs so much punch into a small volume. The book spends little time on frills and is devoted entirely to identifying the problems found with business and professional homepages, and to creating their solutions. ... The book can be read in one sitting, as is helpful for a busy businessperson. The valuable site mistake self-assessment can be completed, and the solutions presented in the book can be put into action immediately."

**— Wayne Hurlbert, Business Blogger, Online Radio Host**

"Home Sweet Home Page by Carma Spence was a very helpful book. It was simple and easy to implement. Already, my homepage has improved and sign-ups for my e-newsletter have gone up. I am looking forward to reading more from this Internet-savvy writer."

**— Elaine Littau, Author, *Nan's Heritage Series***

"If you're an author, speaker, or coach in the process of building or revamping your website or would like to make sure your website has the necessary elements to market yourself and your product, you should consider getting a copy of Carma Spence's book.... Short and succinct, the book describes in an engaging manner the most essential elements of an effective website...."

**— Mayra Calvani, Author**

**Also by Carma Spence**
*Public Speaking Super Powers*
*57 Secrets for Branding Yourself Online*

# HOME *Sweet* HOME PAGE

# HOME
## *Sweet*
# HOME PAGE

How to Fix the 5 Deadly Mistakes
Authors, Speakers, and Coaches Make
with Their Website's Homepage

**2nd Edition**

# CARMA SPENCE

DRAGON *Wyze*
PUBLISHING

**Copyright © 2021 Carma Spence**
Published by DragonWyze Publishing
1314 W 16th Street, Hastings, MN 55033
**www.DragonWyze.com**

DRAGON*Wyze*
PUBLISHING

Printed in the United States of America

Library of Congress Cataloging-in-Publication Data is available upon request.

**Paperback ISBN-10:** 0998531103
**Paperback ISBN-13:** 978-0-9985311-0-6
**Ebook ISBN-10:** 0998531111
**Ebook ISBN-13:** 978-0-9985311-1-3
**First Edition:** December 19, 2009
**Second Edition:** May 18, 2021
**Library of Congress Control Number:** 2020924480

**Limits of Liability and Disclaimer of Warranty**
The author and publisher shall not be liable for your misuse of this material. This book is strictly for informational and educational purposes.

**Warning—Disclaimer**
The purpose of this book is to educate and entertain. The author and/or publisher do not guarantee that anyone following these techniques, suggestions, tips, ideas, or strategies will become successful. The author and/or publisher shall have neither liability nor responsibility to anyone with respect to any loss or damage caused, or alleged to be caused, directly or indirectly by the information contained in this book.

# ACKNOWLEDGMENTS

The encouragement and mentorship of some truly wonderful individuals made this book possible. If it were not for the teaching, guidance, and encouragement of folks like Adam Urbanski, Donna Kozik, Rochelle Walden, Kary Oberbrunner, and Jon Harrow, I don't think I would have arrived at the place I needed to be to write and publish this book or its second edition. Thank you so much!

The many readers of the first edition inspired this second edition. Their encouragement and suggestions motivated me to update and improve this book so that it can help even more authors, speakers, and coaches.

I am also grateful for my husband who always has my back and lovingly puts up with my focused writing binges.

**66**

*"In every art,
beginners must start
with models of those who
have practiced
the same art before
them."*

**– Ruth Whitman**
American Poet, Translator, and Professor

# DEDICATION

I want to thank my mentors for their wisdom and encouragement; my parents for having my back all these years through ups and downs; and my husband for being my best friend, and always supporting me in going after my dreams.

**66**

*"One of the
Internet's strengths
is its ability to hp
consumers
find the right needle in
a digital haystack
of data."*

**– Jared Sandberg**
Reporter, *The Wall Street Journal*

# CONTENTS

# A Special Gift for Readers

I want to reward you for taking the first step toward making your website a more effective tool for growing your business. Therefore, I've created videos, worksheets, checklists, and more additional resources to help you implement the content of this book. You can download your resources here:

CarmaRecommends.com/**hshphandouts**

You're welcome!

# A Note About the Word "Homepage"

When I first wrote *Home Sweet Home Page*, the word was "homepage" was still in flux. You could spell it either as one word or as two. For the title of the book, it worked better as two words, so that's what I went with throughout the book. Things are different now—the correct way to spell homepage is as one word. Because it works better as two in the main title, I left that the same. However, I corrected the spelling everywhere else.

**66**

*"To get through the
hardest journey
we need to take only
one step at a time,
but we must keep on
stepping."*

**– Chinese Proverb**

For a special video related to this chapter, scan the QR code with your phone or go to **CarmaRecommends.com/hshpintroduction**

*Introduction:*

# Online Presence and the Author, Speaker, and Coach

## What Is Online Presence?

The term *online presence* is still in flux. Some people use it to mean the same as "website" … but that is only part of the picture.

According to Michael Cohn of CompuKol Communications, *online presence* is, "any existence of an individual or business that can be found via an online search."

That's a decent definition for the term. However, I think a better one is this: "The visibility or influence of a person or business as reflected by mentions of that person or business throughout the Internet."

You need to understand the implications of that definition.

It doesn't say you have a website. It doesn't say you have social media profiles.

The key to understanding *online presence* is to fully comprehend that it is the **mentions** of you or your business on the web.

You can be the one mentioning you … but other people can mention you as well.

That means you can have an online presence without ever going online yourself. You could be a hermit in a cave and still have a presence online because people talk about you online.

## Why Is Online Presence Important?

As an author, speaker, or coach, it could mean the difference between profitability and closing up shop.

Marketing writer Rachelle Anne Lynn put it quite colorfully this way: "If you don't have a website that customers can find … you are hacking away at your market with an old rusty ax and one hand tied behind your back."

Why would she say this?

The Internet has rapidly become an integral part of our lives.

To illustrate this point, it took radio 38 years to reach 50 million users. But it took the Internet only 4 years to reach that many.

The Internet is woven into the very fabric of the modern way of life. From cell phones to tablets to laptops and beyond, people are constantly accessing the Internet to entertain and inform themselves.

Americans spend more than 60 hours per month online. That's equivalent to spending one month online every year.

Of the North American population, 78.3 percent use the Internet in some way. That's a growth of 151.7 percent between the years 2000 and 2011.

All this Internet use has translated into one very important thing for entrepreneurs: "78 percent of consumers believe it is very important to look up information about people and businesses before deciding to interact or do business with them."

This means without an online presence; you *will* lose business. You are leaving money on the table. You are limiting your career options and income. And, if you want to be in control of that online presence, you need to have a website at its hub.

So how do you leverage this trend in your favor? How do you manage your online presence so that it brings you the readers, clients, projects, and opportunities you desire?

# Your Website's Homepage and Online Presence

The first and most obvious step is having a website. In an ideal world, your website is the hub of your online presence. That means that ultimately, you want all points and pieces of your online presence to point to your website.

Also, your homepage is your most precious and valuable "real estate." The homepage is like a virtual business card, virtual storefront, and virtual greeting card, all wrapped into one.

According to Jakob Nielsen, a User Advocate and principal of the Nielsen Norman Group, the homepage has three main goals:

- To give users information.

- To serve as the top-level navigation for information within the site.

- To tell users the website's purpose.

When it comes to the website of an author, speaker, or coach, I would add one more thing: **To establish credibility, authority, and/or personality**.

I've visited many websites in my meanderings around the web; and one thing that I've noticed is that there are a large number of ineffective homepages out there. Moreover, it seems that most of them belong to solo entrepreneurs, particularly authors, speakers, and coaches.

These websites may accomplish all of Nielsen's goals to some degree, but they often do not accomplish the one I believe is most important—establishing the owner as the go-to person in their field. These websites suffer from what I call the **5 Deadly Mistakes of Homepage Design**:

# 1. Lack of Clarity

I've seen homepages that left me puzzled as to what the website was all about. There were too many things to do and it was not clear what the key purpose of the website was.

## 2. Lack of Professionalism

I'm still surprised by how many people like to use cutesy fonts, free clipart, and clashing colors on their homepage. Some will have distracting background images that make the content difficult to read. Others have noisy animated images or automatic music playing. And still others will have multiple, different calls to action, confusing visitors into saying "No" and leaving.

All these things distract the visitor from the purpose of your website. Even worse, they can increase the load time of your site, so visitors leave before they even see a thing!

## 3. Lack of an Invitation to Continue the Conversation

Most web surfers suffer from short-term memory loss—once they've left a website, they often forget about it, never to return. Therefore, if you want to build a loyal fan base, you must invite visitors to continue the conversation by subscribing to your list. Alas, so many websites of authors, speakers, and coaches either lack this simple tool or de-emphasize it so that it might as well not even be there!

## 4. Lack of a Reason to Continue the Conversation

Long gone is the time when simply offering a web visitor a subscription to your newsletter was enough to get them to give you their name and email address. That is no longer the case. Now you need to give them some immediate, upfront value with an "opt-in incentive." And not only that, you need to tell them why they simply must possess this incentive—you have to sell your freebie!

# 5. Ineffective Copy

As a writer and marketer myself, I understand how hard it can be to write compelling copy that sells *you*. Most of the authors, speakers, and coaches I know are in the business to serve others and have an over-developed sense of humility. This results in some of the worst copy ever written for homepages!

If you can't stand up and tell people why you are the neatest thing since sliced bread, then why should they believe you are? And even those homepages that do have decent copy often have it in the wrong order and don't use appropriate search engine optimization techniques to make this good copy work for them by attracting organic traffic.

That's why I wrote this book—to help authors, speakers, and coaches not only realize what they might be doing wrong, but to show them how to easily fix these mistakes and turn their website into an effective, cost-efficient, business growing tool.

Look at the *5 Deadly Mistakes* and see if you are making any of them with your homepage. There is an easy self-assessment tool at the end of this Introduction to help you. Then flip to that mistake's chapter in the book and discover how to fix it!

**Don't Panic!** You don't have to fix every mistake all at once. Every step you take to improve your homepage will help you grow your business. So take those steps, put one virtual foot in front of the other, and, as the song in the Rankin-Bass animated TV special, *Santa Claus Is Coming to Town* says, "Soon you'll be walkin' out the door!"

# A Note about Off-Page Online Presence

Today, simply having a website is no longer good enough. If you want to manage your online presence and leverage it in your favor, you need to be involved with social media.

More and more people are living a significant portion of their lives online through social media. And it's not just "kids today."

Yes, 96 percent of the under-30 population belong to a social network. However, for Facebook alone, the fastest growing demographic is women between the ages of 55 and 65.

Remember, online presence is more than your website. And it is more than social media. It is also online review sites. It is online forums. It is online directories. It is organizational and association websites. It is YouTube, Amazon, news media websites, RSS feeds and so much more. Consumers—including your readers, event managers who will hire you to speak, and clients—are using search engines to find businesses to purchase from and hire. You want your online presence to show up in those searches.

Nevertheless, despite all this "off-page" online presence that you will need to monitor and manage, the most important part of the puzzle is still your website. If you want your online presence to work for you, to attract readers, clients, projects, and opportunities to you like moths to a flame, you still need to take the most important first step: Create your hub.

Register a domain name and create a website that best represents you to potential readers, clients, partners, employers, and vendors. Also, make sure your website's homepage is compelling to your ideal target market.

Then you can go beyond and develop a presence on the social media sites important to your niche. But that is the topic of another book.

# The Quick 5 Deadly Mistakes Self-Test

Check all those that apply to your homepage. The more you check off, the more likely you are making that deadly mistake.

## Lack of Clarity

- ☐ Several different calls to action
- ☐ No call to action
- ☐ Too many images
- ☐ Too much copy
- ☐ No white space
- ☐ Not sure what you want visitors to do

TOTAL __

## Lack of Professionalism

- ☐ Cutesy fonts
- ☐ Too many different fonts
- ☐ Free clipart
- ☐ More than 5 main colors
- ☐ More than 3 hues of the main color
- ☐ Clashing colors
- ☐ Animated images
- ☐ Automatic audio or video
- ☐ Disorganized content

TOTAL __

## Lack of an Invitation to Continue the Conversation

- ☐ No opt-in form
- ☐ Opt-in form too far down the page
- ☐ Opt-in form is not obvious

TOTAL __

## Lack of a Reason to Continue the Conversation

☐ No opt-in incentive
☐ You only offer a subscription to your e-zine or newsletter
☐ No compelling description of your incentive
☐ No virtual packaging of your opt-in incentive
☐ Not a good match of incentive to your ideal clients

TOTAL __

## Ineffective Copy

☐ "Welcome to my website!"
☐ No compelling headline at the top
☐ Nonsensical tag line
☐ Copy focuses on features
☐ Copy focuses on what you want—not what the visitor wants

TOTAL __

GRAND TOTAL __

How did you do? The higher your score, the more you need to fix your homepage. Focus on those mistakes with the highest scores first.

**66**

*"All you need is a plan, the roadmap, and the courage to press on to your destination."*

**– Earl Nightingale**
American Motivational Speaker

For a special video related to this chapter, scan the QR code with your phone or go to CarmaRecommends.com/hshpmistake1

*Deadly Mistake #1:*

# Not Being Clear on Your Website's Purpose

You've probably heard this before, but if you fail to plan, you are planning to fail. This is very true of your website's homepage, too. If you are not clear about what you are trying to accomplish, how can you expect your visitor to know what to do when they come to your website? If you are not clear on what you are trying to achieve with your website, then you are most likely to achieve nothing at all.

So, you need to create a mission and vision statement for your website, most likely it will be very similar to the mission and vision statement for your business. You do have those, right?

Well, just in case you don't, here are the steps you need to take to create them.

# Who Is Your Target Market?

Do you have a picture of your ideal client in your head? Have you created a list of qualities that this person possesses? What are the types of things that members of your target market have in common? For example, I serve authors, speakers, coaches, and other information-based service professionals. However, not all people in those groups are ideal clients for me. I've added another layer of criteria to my "ideal client." The people I love to serve and serve the best, have these qualities as well:

- A quirky sense of humor—without that, they probably just wouldn't "get" me anyway.

- An active inner child—who else will understand my undying love for Tigger?

- Creative and imaginative—I find it too difficult to work with people who don't nurture their creative spark.

- Open-minded and ready to take action—I don't have time to work with people who will fight me all the way and won't take the actions necessary to benefit from my advice.

Now, does that mean I won't take on clients who don't fit these criteria to the letter? Of course not. However, because I have this quirky, imaginative, and action-oriented professional in my mind, it makes it easier for me to create marketing messages that will speak to that type of person.

Therefore, first, you need to be clear on whom it is that you serve. Then you need to understand what keeps them up at night.

# What Does Your Target Market Want... That Only You Can Help Them With?

Your homepage must speak to your target market's greatest fears and most cherished desires. Therefore, you have to know what they are. And you need to focus on those specific fears and desires that only you can help them with.

Now, that doesn't mean you have to be the only one in your field providing that type of service. For example, there are plenty of self-improvement authors, inspirational speakers and life coaches out there. But each individual brings to those services a uniqueness, a special something that is born out of their life's journey, their passions, and their personality. And therefore, each individual will attract clients and customers who most resonate with that particular combination of qualities that make that author, speaker, or coach distinctive.

For example, my favorite author is Ray Bradbury—I've even met him in person. However, many people out there are not fond of his poetic, dreamy style of writing. And that's O.K. They aren't his target market!

*Keep this in mind*: If someone does not like or "get" what you have to offer, that's O.K. That person is not in your target market and you wouldn't want to work with them anyway! So don't be afraid to let your personality shine in your marketing materials and your website—by doing this you are more likely to attract your ideal clients and weed out the people you were not meant to serve anyway.

# What Is Your Website's Job?

Now, let's get clear on the purpose of your website. This may seem like a silly thing to think about—your website's purpose is to grow your business, right?

Yes, but in what way? Do you want your website to increase your visibility? Establish your brand? Make a sale? Collect visitor information? Establish your expertise?

Depending on your answer, your homepage can look completely different! So let's talk about the different kinds of websites you can have.

## The Branding Website

A branding website focuses on establishing and building a brand. A brand is the perception of a company, product, or service. It is the essence of what will be delivered or experienced through that company, product, or service. It is much larger than a logo, tag line, or jingle. It is an emotion, and more.

For example, Nordstrom's brand is centered on exquisite customer service. Wal-Mart's brand is focused on low prices. Pepperidge Farms' brand is focused on old-fashioned taste and quality. Do you see a trend here? None of these brands truly communicate what they sell. They communicate a value or emotion attached to or achieved by what they sell.

Therefore a branding website needs to communicate this essence, this feeling, this nebulous perception. And it does this through color and image choice, as well as word selection. A website that is heavy on ambiance and light on information is a branding website.

Most authors, speakers, and coaches don't need a branding website *per se*. However, their brand is communicated throughout their website.

## The Sales Website

As the name suggests, a sales website is focused on making a sale. It can be something as simple as a sales page—a sales letter posted on the Internet—or as complex as an e-commerce site like Amazon.com.

Most authors, speakers, and coaches are best served by having individual sales pages rather than sales websites. Their homepage is usually used to establish expertise and forge a relationship, rather than make a sale right away.

## The Relationship Builder Website

The focus of a relationship builder website is on community. This type of website seeks to establish an ongoing relationship with the visitor and therefore provides a variety of ways to interact with the site and the site's owner.

Membership sites, whether free or fee-based, are the quintessential relationship-building websites. Again, authors, speakers, and coaches usually don't have this level of relationship-building on their website. And if they have a membership site, it is secondary to their main website. Most authors, speakers, and coaches have moved to Facebook and LinkedIn groups for this purpose.

## The Expert Library Website

Business blogs are the most common type of expert library website. These sites focus on establishing the expertise of the site owner by providing a library of information the visitor can peruse for free (and sometimes for a fee).

This is often the most effective type of site for authors, speakers, and coaches if it is done the right way.

## The Combination Website

More often than not you'll want your website to accomplish several of the above-mentioned goals. And that's O.K.—as long as you are clear on the purpose of the *homepage* and keep that page focused on one primary goal.

A combination site usually chooses one of the above purposes as its dominant focus of the homepage, while having a secondary purpose woven in. For example, a common combination homepage for authors, speakers, and coaches establishes the individual's brand by communicating through copy and imagery the person's branding qualities, such as compassion, fun, courage (whatever they may be) while at the same time, having a clear "call to action" to join the mailing list (the secondary purpose). The navigation menu points visitors to the sales pages and blog (expert library).

Although the website, as a whole, may accomplish all the purposes eventually, the homepage should be focused on no more than *two*.

# A Note about Website Platform

There are basically two types of website platforms—static and dynamic. A static website is composed of simple, independent pages linked together. A dynamic website is composed of pages that are dynamically created as you visit each page from master templates and a content database.

Your choice of platform depends on how often you will need to update your pages and how big you think your website will grow, as well as your technical knowledge.

However, these days, using dynamic web platforms, such as WordPress, to create sales pages with improved search engine optimization features is the standard.

There was a time when static websites were much more common. People would use them for single sales pages or mini-websites composed of a small number of pages.

There are services now that easily create these one-off landing pages, with little or no technical knowledge required on your part. For some recommendations go to:

CarmaRecommends.com/**hshpresources**

Larger websites demand a content management system—or it becomes too difficult to manage all the pages and make changes to the look and feel behind the scenes.

Also, if you are not well-versed in HTML and you don't want to depend on a webmaster to make all your changes for you, you should look into using one of the more user-friendly content management systems based on the blogging platform that are available, such as WordPress, Drupal, and Joomla.

# The Fix

The fix for the **First Deadly Mistake** is to get clear on:

- Who your target market is
- What they want
- What you can help them with
- How you want to present yourself on the homepage

You should also get specific on your goals so that you can measure your success and know when you need to go back and do some more fine-tuning. For example, how many leads do you want to generate? How much money in sales? In what time frame? Define, specifically, what you want to see for you to feel that your website is a success.

You can download worksheets and other resources to help you implement the concepts in this and other, chapters here:

CarmaRecommends.com/**hshphandouts**

**66**

*"Successful
websites are for
their readers,
not their owners."*

**– Thomas Umstattd, Jr.**
Author, Speaker, Podcaster, Blogger

For a special video related to this chapter, scan the QR code with your phone or go to **CarmaRecommends.com/hshpmistake2**

*Deadly Mistake #2:*

# Unprofessional First Impression

Many authors, speakers, and coaches spend a lot of time working virtually—communicating with their clients via telephone, Skype, Zoom, email, and other methods that don't require them to leave their home office (speakers, possibly a little less often), so they do not need to be personally presentable all the time.

However, this is *not* the case for your website. Your website needs to be presentable 24 hours a day, seven days a week.

And there are quite a few elements that can go into the first impression of your website.

- Your domain name
- Your navigation
- The general layout
- The fonts you use

- The colors you use
- Your use of images
- Your copy

Let's look at each one and how to make sure they give a professional first impression.

## What Does Your Domain Say about Your Business?

Domain names are to websites as titles are to novels ... and a little bit more. Your domain should accomplish several things:

- Clearly identify what your business or website is about
- Capture interest in visiting the website
- Help with search engine optimization
- Be easy to understand and remember
- Support your brand

The obvious choice for authors, speakers, and coaches is your name: JaneDoe.com or JaneDoeBooks.com or CoachJane.com or something like that. This type of domain satisfies many of the above criteria, and if one of the goals of your website is to brand you and build name recognition, you should most assuredly use a name-based domain. It clearly identifies you as the core product; as you become known, it will capture interest; it supports search engine optimization of your name; it is easy to remember (if your name is easy to remember); and it supports your brand.

However, if you are trying to build a brand that you can later sell or bequeath to your children or grandchildren, you might want to go a different route and purchase a domain that describes your service or is the name of a product. For example, I have "publicspeakingsuperpowers.com" because that is the name of one of my books, and I want to keep the bulk of my public speaking content separate from the content of my name-based website.

In an ideal world, you want to have a .com domain. This is the extension that is most recognized by Internet users as the one for professional websites. You also want to avoid hyphens, unless it will make the domain easier to understand or remember.

Take, for example, speedofart.com. This domain can be read two ways: "Speed of Art" or "Speedo Fart." The former is the intended meaning—hyphens would have made it clearer. So, before you purchase that domain, look at other words that might be lurking in the combination.

*Note*: There have been many unfortunate domains that existed when I first wrote this book. Most of them have gone offline, but if you want to find them, search your favorite browser for "unfortunate domains."

## Is Your Website Easy to Navigate?

If your visitors find it too frustrating to navigate your website to find what they want or need, they will often leave, never to return. So make your navigation clear and uncluttered. Divide your content into groups or buckets, with navigational links only to the top-level page. Three to seven buckets is a good range to aim for.

Other strategies include:

## Break up your navigation

Not everyone is going to be interested in your "Media Room" or "Privacy Policy" pages, so you don't need to include them in your main navigation. Put them at the bottom of the page where those who truly want to find them can, while at the same time remaining unobtrusive.

## Have duplicate navigation

Some people prefer a top navigation bar, while others look for a navigational sidebar. You satisfy both of these types of visitors by having both! You'd be surprised how many visitors will easily find their preferred navigation location and not even know the other is there.

# Essential Pages for Authors, Speakers, and Coaches

In my philosophy, all authors should be speakers and coaches; all speakers should be authors and coaches; and all coaches should be authors and speakers. To have a thriving expertise-based business you need all three elements. That said, one will more than likely be primary over the others. With that in mind, here are the essential pages that need to be a part of your website and should be included in your navigation.

## About/Bio Page

This page lets visitors know your story and why you are the person they should be considering. However, your bio should always keep the reader in mind. Let your website visitors know all the things they should (and want) to know about you in an engaging manner. This page can also include testimonials and should include a good, professionally taken headshot of you.

This page is especially important for authors and other experts because it is often the page that draws the second most traffic.

## Books/Products/Services

Here is where you let visitors know what you have to offer. If you offer a lot, this could be several pages rather than one. However, only the top-level link needs to be in the navigation.

## Events

Where are you speaking next? Where have you spoken before? People want to know this information because it lets them know if you have the authority or not. Of course, if you have nothing to put on this page yet, you can leave it off until you do.

## Blog

According to Hubspot, a company with expertise in content marketing, websites that have a blog get 55 percent more traffic than those that don't. Use your blog to share your expertise. If you can share good quality, valuable information at least once a month, you'll reap the benefits of having a blog.

## Media Kit & Press Coverage

A media kit provides information that the press can use to better write about you. Here is where you provide images of your book and product covers, headshots, short and long versions of your bio, suggested interview questions, and any other information that will help the media cover you on their shows, on their pages, and through the airwaves.

A press coverage page highlights mentions of you in the media. Here is where you will display clips of you appearing on radio, podcasts, and TV, as well as mentions of you in newspapers, magazines, and online outlets.

## Contact

Your contact page should be separate from other pages. On this page, you should include your phone number, email address, mailing address, and other ways to get in touch with you. Be strategic—and safe. Maintain a balance between being reachable and offering too much information. You can always get a P.O. Box to protect your home address.

Since this page needs to be easily accessible on every page of your website, including it in your primary navigation is a good idea.

# Is Your Website Easy to Look At?

Related to navigation, what does the general layout of your site say about its purpose and content? Obviously, a branding website is going to look different from an expert library website. Is your layout congruent with the purpose and function of your website?

Other things that affect the "easy on the eyes" qualities of your website are font and color choice. Here are some basic rules:

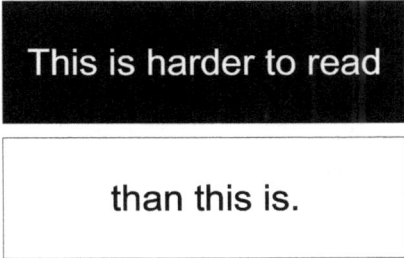

**This is harder to read**

**than this is.**

- Dark fonts on light backgrounds are easier to read than light fonts on dark backgrounds.

- *Serif* fonts, such as Times, may be easier to read in print but are often less easy to read online. But this is also a subjective thing—I find *sans serif* fonts like Century Gothic easier to read, while I know others who prefer *serif* fonts. Choose a font that supports the overall look and feel you want for your website.

  A *serif* font, like Times, has little curly cues—or *serifs*—on it. A *sans serif* font is "without *serif*." I'm using a *serif* font for the body of this book and a *sans serif* font for titles, subheads, and footnotes.

  **This is a serif font**
  **This is a sans serif font**

- Use standard fonts for the majority of your text and save the fancy fonts for graphics. Using silly fonts, like Comic Sans, will just undercut your credibility and call your professionalism into question.

- Use a balance of warm and cool colors, and don't use too many different colors. Usually, a color palette of three primary colors supported by up to three secondary colors is the most you should have. Secondary colors are usually different hues of the primary colors. You can use these colors to emphasize headlines and they should complement the colors in your header graphic. If you are unsure of what colors go well together, you can find plenty of resources on the web to help you. Color Combos, **www.colorcombos.com**, is a good resource that allows you to experiment with different color combinations interactively and provides you with the HEX codes you or your web designer will need.

## Is It Clear What You Want Your Visitor To Do?

Of course, if your website is going to be effective, it needs to be clear about what you want the visitor to do. Your choices in all the above need to be focused on, and supportive of, this one call to action. Professional websites have a clear purpose and tell their visitors in no uncertain terms exactly what they should do next: click, buy, subscribe, download, etc.

## Is Your Website "Well-Groomed"?

Is your homepage neat and tidy or messy and cluttered? White space is your friend. You don't want to overwhelm your visitor. Are the graphics congruent with the image you want it to portray and the words you use? Are you using the right words in the right order? Are they broken up into easy-to-read chunks, using headlines, subheads, and bullets?

# The Fix

The fix for the **Second Deadly Mistake** is:

- Have a clear and easy-to-understand domain name

- Make your website easy to navigate

- Use a crisp, clean design that supports your overall brand and message

- Make your call to action obvious

- Use graphics sparingly, and only use those that are relevant to the text

You might want to look at websites around the web and jot down what you like about them, and what doesn't work so well for you. Ask your clients what they like. Before finalizing your design, get a second opinion. Trust me on this … it is easy to miss things that are blatantly obvious when you are too close to them.

You can download worksheets and other resources to help you implement the concepts in this, and other, chapters here:

CarmaRecommends.com/**hshphandouts**

**66**

*"Your ability to
communicate
is an important tool
in your pursuit of
your goals,
whether it is with
your family,
your co-workers,
or your clients and
customers."*

**– Les Brown**
Motivational Speaker

For a special video related to this chapter, scan the QR code with your phone or go to
CarmaRecommends.com/hshpmistake3

*Deadly Mistake #3:*

# Not Collecting Visitor Information

This deadly mistake not only can ruin the effectiveness of your homepage, but it can also kill your business! If you don't have a list of prospects and clients that you can communicate with regularly, then you don't have a business.

Yet, I've seen author after speaker after coach have websites that don't have an opt-in form, have an unobtrusive ("introverted") opt-in form, or an opt-in form that is far down the page. Ask yourself the following questions … and if your answer is no, fix it to yes!

## Do You Have an Opt-In Form?

You can't collect the names and email addresses of visitors if you don't have an opt-in form somewhere on your website. Your email marketing software or service will give you the code you need to create an opt-in form, but you need to take it one step further and surround that code with an eye-catching form, which I'll talk about later in this chapter.

In some cases, it is best to have an opt-in invitation button that opens a new window or pop-up that has the actual form. There is some evidence that this increase sign-up rates. Experiment to discover what works best with your audience.

## Is Your Opt-In Form "Above the Fold"?

Next, you want to make sure that your opt-in form is one of the first things your visitors see. You want it to be "above the fold"—that is people should not have to scroll down the page to get to it. Moreover, it should stand out from the rest of the content on the page.

## Does Your Opt-In Form Make a Compelling Offer?

There was a time when providing a subscription to a free monthly e-zine was enough of an incentive for entering your name and email address in an opt-in form. But, with the rise of SPAM and the increasing deluge of emails that every one of us gets, this is no longer the case.

Now you need to offer your visitors a compelling opt-in gift—something that speaks to their fears and/or desires and adds value to their life or business. Also, the opt-in needs to be quick and easy to consume. People are more likely to opt-in for a checklist than an e-book.

Compelling offers can include:

- A targeted report on a topic of interest
- An audio recording
- A video recording
- An assessment tool or quiz
- A template
- A checklist
- A webinar
- A resource list

Many of these can be downloadable, so your subscriber can have instant gratification. Which lead magnet that will serve you best depends on your target market and what is compelling to them. For example, corporate audiences respond better to "white papers" or reports, whereas entrepreneurs respond better to checklists and templates.

Other compelling offers are becoming more common—physical products where the subscriber only pays for the shipping. These can be CDs, DVDs, books, or something else relevant to your audience. The thought process is, if the subscriber had to pay money to get the gift, he or she is already "in the habit" of paying you money and will be more likely to purchase your products or services in the future.

Educational videos and video series are also on the rise. Again, you need to know what your target market is most likely to respond to.

Regardless of what your opt-in incentive may be, you must sell it so that the subscriber understands its value and is compelled to exchange something—their name and email address or the cost of shipping—for it.

## Is Your Opt-In Form Visually Compelling?

Again, all of the above will be for naught if your website visitors don't even notice that it's there! Your opt-in form should stand out from the rest of your website.

You can do this by using bright red arrows and colorful depictions of your opt-in incentive. It can use a slightly different design style than the rest of the site. Or it can be a prominent part of the homepage design.

Regardless of how you accomplish this goal, the key is making it blatantly obvious that you would like the visitor to subscribe to your opt-in list!

Many autoresponder and landing page services make this easy by providing a selection of beautiful templates you can use. If not, get your web designer to create one for you.

# The Fix

The fix for the **Third Deadly Mistake** is:

- Have an opt-in form
- Place it near the top of your homepage
- Give visitors a compelling reason to opt-in
- Make your opt-in form stand out and get noticed

Of course, this entire chapter assumes you have an email marketing service or software set up. Without this essential business tool, your opt-in form won't work and if you do get it to work, the time and effort required to maintain your list will be prohibitive.

Not to mention, using an email marketing service helps you stay compliant with Anti-Spam laws. Moreover, you have no excuse not to use one; there are a few available that are free when your list is small. For a list of suggestions, visit:

CarmaRecommends.com/**hshpresources**

You can download worksheets and other resources to help you implement the concepts in this, and other, chapters here:

CarmaRecommends.com/**hshphandouts**

**66**

*"Internet mailing lists are like Fox television shows. They have really cool previews, and they get you all excited about them, but they just don't live up to their promises."*

**– John Dobbin**
Blogger

For a special video related to this chapter, scan the QR code with your phone or go to
**CarmaRecommends.com/hshpmistake4**

*Deadly Mistake #4:*

# Not Having a Compelling Opt-in Incentive

I've touched on this topic a little earlier in this book, but it truly is that important. You can't just put up any opt-in incentive and expect to grow your list of raving fans. You need to "sell" your incentive and then deliver on the goods. Or, as John Dobbin suggests, you don't want to be like a Fox television show!

## The "Free Taste"

The best opt-in incentives provide subscribers with a sample of your products or services. It's kind of like when you go to the grocery store and they are giving out free tastes of some new product. You try it and, if you like it, you buy it.

That's the idea behind your opt-in incentive. You are giving your prospects a low-risk way to sample your services to see if they like what you have to offer. Your incentive should highlight your expertise and be an expression of your brand. It should give them an idea of what it might be like to work with you.

## Is Your Opt-In Incentive in a Format Your Target Market Prefers?

There are three main learning styles: audio, visual, and kinesthetic. Most likely, you will attract prospects predominantly from one of those three styles. Therefore, provide your free taste in a format that works best for that style of learning:

- *Audio learners* prefer audio gifts in download or CD format, as well as videos.

- *Visual learners* prefer video gifts, as well as charts, graphs, and infographics.

- *Kinesthetic learners* prefer gifts they can interact with, such as quizzes, assessments, guidebooks, and checklists.

*Even better:* Offer an opt-in incentive that can appeal to more than one kind of learning style. Or offer a range of incentives in different formats. Remember, you will attract prospects from all three learning styles and will need to create products and services that meet all their learning style needs if you want to have a thriving business.

# Is Your Opt-In Incentive an Integral Part of Your Marketing Funnel?

Leads & Prospects

Free or Low-Cost Products

Mid-Range Priced Products & Services

High-Ticket Products & Services

Not only should your opt-in incentive be a sample of your products and services, but it should also be a sales tool that guides subscribers to purchase those products and services. It should be a part of your marketing funnel.

As illustrated above, you can think of your business as being like a funnel, with the lowest-priced items at the wide-open top and your high-ticket items at the bottom of the funnel. This is a visual representation of the flow of prospects through your business.

For example, let's say that you attract 100 prospects with your opt-in incentive. Not all of those prospects will become clients. Let's say 50 of them move on to buy your mid-range products and services. Do you see how the funnel has gotten narrower? Out of those 50, some will not move on to buy your highest ticket items. Again, the funnel gets narrower.

Your opt-in incentive needs to both attract enough prospects to fill the funnel and contain enough value that it convinces a good percentage of them to take the next step and purchase something from you. It should also be focused enough to be especially attractive to your ideal prospects while discouraging everyone else.

## Does Your "Opt-In Incentive" Have Eye-Catching Packaging?

Remember earlier in this chapter when I mentioned the three learning styles? Guess which one is the most common? About 40 to 65 percent of the population favors the visual learning style. Therefore, they will respond to visual images more than mere words.

Think about it. When you're perusing the bookstore, what makes you pick up one book over the other? When in the grocery store and are looking for a product you haven't purchased before, what makes you choose one product over the other? In both cases, it most likely was the packaging. Alas, most people do "judge a book by its cover."

Of course, your opt-in incentive is most likely a digital product and has no real packaging. However, it can have virtual packaging—a graphical image that represents what your product might look like if it were a physical product.

Therefore, give your digital download a cover. Make it 3D, if you can. Give your visitors something they can see and "virtually" touch to encourage them to get your gift.

# The Fix

The fix for the **Fourth Deadly Mistake** is:

- Offer a free taste of your products and/or services in exchange for visitors' names and email addresses
- Provide this free taste in a format your target market prefers
- Market your products and services within the opt-in incentive
- Give your opt-in incentive some visual bling with virtual packaging

If you don't know how to create this packaging yourself using a software application such as Photoshop, some free websites can help you do this in a basic way. I've listed some here:

CarmaRecommends.com/**hshpresources**

However, as in physical products, how professional your packaging looks can make a big difference, so you might consider hiring a designer or using a paid service to create these images for you. Fiverr is a good resource for affordable graphic services.

You can download worksheets and other resources to help you implement the concepts in this, and other, chapters here:

CarmaRecommends.com/**hshphandouts**

**66**

*"I don't build in order to have clients.
I have clients in order to build."*

**– Ayn Rand**
Russian-American Novelist
and Philosopher

*Deadly Mistake #5:*

# Poor Use of Copy Optimization

At its best, bad copy is ineffective. At its worst, it can destroy your reputation. Now, most author, speaker, and coach websites I've seen haven't suffered from the latter, but they certainly have suffered from the former!

Jakob Nielsen considers emphasizing "what your site offers that's of value to users, and how your services differ from those of key competitors" one of the most important issues in homepage design. But so many websites fall short on this point.

They use ineffective copy that is poorly written and poorly organized. In many websites I've seen, the most important, attention-grabbing information is often far down the page. And oftentimes, the copy doesn't flow logically. Here are some tips to help you diagnose ineffective copy on your website and fix it so that it works much better.

# Do You Have Strong Headlines?

Your headlines are going to be the first text your website visitor will read. The content of your header or first headline will determine if the visitor stays to read some more, opts into your list, or just moves on to the next website. So, you need your headline to be strong and indicate a benefit the visitor will gain by associating with you. Here are six basic headline formulas you can use to draw readers in:

1. **State your biggest promise or benefit.**
*Example:* Double Your Email List in 90 Days

2. **Identify your ideal prospect.**
*Example:* Helping Entrepreneurs Achieve Social Media Success

3. **The news headline.**
*Example:* Announcing a New Way to Manage Your Books

4. **The quick and easy solution.**
*Example:* Write a Business Book in 30 Days or Less

5. **The provocative question.**
*Example:* Are you making these relationship mistakes?

6. **Evoke curiosity.**
*Example:* 5 Mistakes Authors Make When Writing Their First Book

There are many more formulas you can follow, but these six are a great way to get started.

*Another tip:* Know what your Unique Selling Proposition, or USP, is and focus your headline on that. You want your headline to grab your visitor's attention and draw them into your site, so capture their attention with your chief and most excellent benefit—your USP!

# Do You Have Enticing Subheads?

Your subhead is like a transition from your headline to your copy. It should support your headline and hook your reader. A subhead can go into more detail about what you suggested in the headline, but not as much detail as your main copy.

Subheads also act as a way to state key points throughout longer copy. They are your way of letting "scanners"—people who scan, rather than read, copy for key information—know what you're talking about in the rest of the copy and enticing them to read what you have to say. Brian Clark of **copyblogger.com** suggests that when writing subheads, you shouldn't "think in terms of subheads, think sub-benefits" instead.

For example, the subheads I'm using in this book work because they ask questions that encourage you to read on for the answer. They also suggest benefits you'll gain by reading my book when you see them in the Table of Contents.

# Is Your Copy Written in an Appropriate Voice?

All writing has a voice—even copywriting. And effective sales copy—which is what you must have on your homepage, even if what you are selling is free—is transparent and persuasive. For most authors, speakers, and coaches, the voice you use in your sales copy should be authentic to who you are and the way you provide your services. If you are not loud, boisterous, and hype-y, then your sales copy shouldn't be either.

Some good advice I've received about copywriting is to write your first draft as if you were writing a letter to a friend, someone who is representative of your target market.

If you are truly passionate about what you are offering, let this enthusiasm shine through!

# Is Your Copy Easy to Read Online?

Here is where so many people fail! Reading pixels on a screen is very different from reading ink on a page. Because the computer screen is flashing very rapidly, so fast that the conscious mind is unaware of it, reading on the screen is harder on the eyes than reading off a printed page. For this reason, people tend to scan online copy rather than read it. Therefore, you have to format the copy for easy scanning.

## Break up the copy with subheads.

Start each new thought with a subhead that summarizes that thought. Use "sub-benefits" as your sub-headlines. "Scanners" will read these subheads to see what the gist of the content is.

## Use bullet points.

People love lists. Therefore, when you use bullets, you are more likely to get people to read your copy. Also, bulleted lists create more white space around your text, making it easier to read.

## Use a decent sized font.

Many websites use small fonts that are hard to read. Even worse, I've noticed a trend for this small font size to be in a medium gray color, rather than black! Talk about making it hard to read!

## Be aware of color choice.

As I've mentioned earlier in this book, dark colors on a light background are easier to read. Save your bright colors for emphasis, headlines, and subheads. And stay away from boldly colored backgrounds.

## Keep paragraphs short.

Large blocks of text give readers the perception that what they have to read will be cumbersome and difficult. Therefore, break up your paragraphs so that most of them are five lines long or less.

Follow these tips and your copy will be much more readable online!

# Are You Using the Proper HTML Tags for Search Engine Optimization?

When a search engine is evaluating your webpage to rank it for search results, it looks at the HTML tags that format each bit of text. Headlines that use the headline tags ("h1", "h2", "h3", etc.) are given more weight than other copy. Many website owners miss out on this little bit of search engine optimization by using bold tags (<strong></strong>) instead. Correct this mistake and you can improve your ranking in search engine results.

*Another tip*: Use keywords in your headlines as much as possible. This may not be feasible on your homepage, where your priorities are more on grabbing reader attention, but keep it in mind. When a search engine sees keywords between header tags, they have more weight than when they are between paragraph ("p") tags.

*NOTE*: If this HTML talk is a little above your head, make sure your web person knows you want to use this optimization technique. He or she will understand what to do.

# The Fix

The fix for the **Fifth Deadly Mistake** is:

- Write strong, benefit-focused headlines

- Use subheads that focus on "sub-benefits"

- Write your copy in a voice that is congruent with who you are, and is appropriate for your target market

- Break up your copy with short paragraphs and bullets to make it easier to read

- Use H tags to improve search engine optimization

Before you write your copy, you should have a clear idea of what your USP, or Unique Selling Proposition, is. What makes what you have to offer different from other, similar products and services? For authors, speakers, and coaches, this USP is often grounded in your distinctive personality and life journey. Embrace who you are—and leverage it for success.

You can download worksheets and other resources to help you implement the concepts in this, and other, chapters here:

CarmaRecommends.com/**hshphandouts**

**66**

*"Whosoever desires constant success must change his conduct with the times."*

**– Niccolo Machiavelli**
Italian Politician, Writer and Author

For a special video related to this chapter, scan the QR code with your phone or go to CarmaRecommends.com/hshpmistake6

**BONUS—** *Deadly Mistake #6:*

# Not Keeping Up with the Times

Although much that I included in my first edition of this book has not changed, some things have. There is some new information, and some other information is no longer true. Therefore, to keep up with the times, I published this second edition.

The same is true of your website and its homepage. Methods and techniques that work one year may not work a couple of years later, so the effectiveness of your homepage drops if you don't regularly spruce it up. This goes for your entire website as well.

## Is Your Website Mobile-Friendly?

This was once not very important. However, these days most people carry a mobile device from which they will access your website.

In fact, as of 2016, about 60 percent of searches were made from mobile devices, and that number is increasing.

Google, the most popular search engine, favors mobile-friendly websites over those that aren't. In fact, it will sometimes penalize sites that are not mobile-friendly, relegating them to the third (or more) results page. You can see that having a mobile-friendly website is pretty darn important.

So make sure your homepage functions just as well on a smartphone and tablet as it does on a laptop and desktop computer.

## When Was the Last Time You Updated the Look and Feel of Your Website?

Given that technology is changing so rapidly, it is recommended that you make sure your website works on modern devices and browsers at least every other year, if not more often.

Also, you should be updating the look of your website at least every three or four years. Design trends change, too, and if your website looks "old fashioned," it reduces your credibility.

This is why I recommend that you use a content management system (CMS), such as WordPress. These CMSs have mobile-friendly themes that are easy to install and often are easy to modify so that they match your branding. Once you have your content inside a CMS, you can update the theme, which manages the look and feel of your site, with relative ease whenever you choose.

# Are You Keeping Your Content Clean?

If you are a regular blogger, doing a periodic content audit can be critical to maintaining the relevance of your website in search engine results. A content audit is when you take an inventory of your website's content and make sure that it is still relevant to the purpose of your website and is up-to-date.

Some content marketing purists would also advise you to delete all content that is not relevant or up-to-date, while others will tell you just to add a note about why it is no longer relevant or accurate. As I write this book, I'm going through my first content audit and am planning on deleting all irrelevant content and updating all out-of-date content. That way I can ensure that my content is focused. I feel no need to overwhelm my visitors with content for content's sake. And neither should you.

Also, if you are using WordPress, you may have noticed that you can now mark content as being a "cornerstone article." This is a feature that allows you to let search engines know which pages are the most important ones on your website. Cornerstone articles contain information that exactly reflects your business. You can read more about this type of content at

**yoast.com/cornerstone-article-content-type**

# Does Your Site Have Broken Links?

Broken links can damage your SEO. Make sure that you are keeping your links up-to-date. Again, if you have WordPress, this can be easily done. Simply install a plugin that checks for broken links and emails you when it finds any. I use such a plugin for all my websites, and it has saved me a lot of hassle and work.

# The Fix

The fix for the **Sixth Deadly Mistake** is:

- Check to make sure your website works on mobile devices, particularly phones and tablets

- Schedule regular website facelifts every three to four years

- Conduct a content audit every couple of years to make sure all content is relevant and up-to-date

- Install software to notify you when links on your website become broken

I know it can be a hassle to keep up with the times, but it is a business task you can't afford to ignore.

You can download worksheets and other resources to help you implement the concepts in this, and other, chapters here:

CarmaRecommends.com/**hshphandouts**

**66**

*"What separates
design from art is
that design
is meant to be
functional."*

**– Cameron Moll**
User Experience Leader and Strategist

# *Conclusion*

I've had several writing mentors tell me that I should always follow the rules of grammar ... except when I shouldn't. It is the same way with the **6 Deadly Mistakes**. However, when you do break these "rules of an effective homepage," you should do so consciously, on purpose, and for a strategic reason.

There will be times when having an opt-in form above the fold will be counter to the purpose of your homepage. There will be times when you want your website to look "unprofessional." But you should make these decisions consciously and in support of your clear goal for the homepage. (You should never make Mistake #1!)

Jakob Nielsen says, "Improving your homepage multiplies the entire website's business value." I hope that the tips I provided in this book have helped you increase the business value of your website, attract more subscribers for your list, and grow your base of fans.

**66**

*"Somewhere there
is a map
of how it can be
done."*

**– Ben Stein**
Actor, Writer, Commentator, Lawyer,
Teacher, and Humorist

# Appendices

**66**

*"Finding your style is like putting puzzle pieces together."*

**– Lara Spencer**
American Television Journalist

*Appendix A:*

# 5 Key Components for an Effective Homepage

## 1. An Effective Tag Line

Your tagline should catch attention, clarify the purpose of your business, and engage your ideal clients, readers, or audience members.

Ideally, your tagline should be no more than one sentence long and it doesn't need to be a slogan. Some good examples include:

- *Example 1*: Relationship coaching for smart, professional women
- *Example 2*: Content strategy for women entrepreneurs
- *Example 3*: Business mastery training with heart

Each of these tag lines makes it very clear what each business is all about. This is the primary purpose of your tag line.

## 2. Title Tags

When you visit a website, look at the top of your browser window, and you'll see some text that should describe the page you're on.

This text is created by the "TITLE" tags in the code for the page and is used by search engines and bookmark lists. You want this title tag to include your company name and/or keywords. Avoid starting the title tag with "The" and leave "Welcome to" out. Your Webmaster will know how to do this, and if you're using WordPress, this is automatically created for you.

## 3. A Link to the About Page

At some point, your website visitor will probably want to know more about you. Therefore, you need to have an "About" page and place the link in an easy-to-find location on the homepage. You don't need to put this information on the homepage—in fact, I strongly discourage it. This information does not need to take up your precious front-page virtual real estate. The primary navigation bar is the most common place for this.

## 4. Primary Navigation

If you have a large website—or even one that is not so large—you are going to have many pages a person can visit. But you don't need to show them all on the homepage. Try to limit the navigational links to three to seven major sections. The fewer options your visitor has, the easier it will be for them to navigate your site.

# 5. Use Meaningful Graphics

I must admit, I struggle with this one sometimes—I like things to look pretty. But when it comes right down to it, if the image does not fully support the text, it has no reason to be there. Pictures may be worth a 1,000 words, but as one of my mentors, Adam Urbanski, says, you have no control over which 1,000 words they are. "Images are powerful communicators when they show items of interest to users," wrote Jakob Nielsen, "but will backfire if they seem frivolous or irrelevant." So make sure the images underscore, support, and are relevant to the copy on your homepage.

To view a video explanation of the 5 key components, go to:

CarmaRecommends.com/**hshp5keycomponents**

**66**

*"The key to wisdom is knowing the right questions."*

**– John A. Simone, Sr.**

# *Appendix B:*

# The 6 Questions You Need to Answer with Your Website

A visitor comes to your website. Before they will entrust their name, email, address, or money to you, you need to answer these six questions they will ask—either consciously or unconsciously.

## 1. Do I trust you?

You have to establish your trustworthiness. This can be accomplished in several ways, including adding a simple statement that you won't rent or sell their information. It is also a good idea to have a link to a privacy policy somewhere on the page.

If you are collecting money through your website, making sure it is secure with an SSL certificate is a good idea. Badges from credibility companies, such as the Better Business Bureau, help, too.

Testimonials and reviews can also help with building trust.

## 2. Do I believe you?

Jef I. Richards of the Journal of Interactive Advertising once said, "I believe 'credibility' is one of the biggest issues yet to be addressed by Internet advertisers." Your website visitors are going to be jaded, so you are going to have to establish credibility before they will open their hearts (and wallets) to you. This starts with your website. It is continued once they join your list.

## 3. Do you understand my needs?

People want to feel understood. If they don't feel you understand them, they are not going to trust that your solution will solve their problem. Therefore, you need to be clear about your target market and what their needs and concerns are.

## 4. What's in it for me?

It is easy to get caught up in the features of your products and the services you provide that you forget to let people know what the benefits are. You have to stress the benefits, or you will lose the opportunity to continue the conversation or make the sale.

## 5. What do you want from me?

Remember the call to action! If you don't tell people what you want them to do, they won't do it.

# 6. Is it worth it?

You must make sure that your website visitor understands the value of what you have to offer. You can do this by talking about the benefits, sharing testimonials and case studies, and including bonus items.

For a deeper dive, grab your copy of the Six Questions program, available at:

CarmaRecommends.com/**sixquestions**

**66**

*"No man can rise to fame and fortune without carrying others along with him."*

**— Napoleon Hill**
Author, *Think and Grow Rich*

# More Support and Information

If you'd like to dive deeper into the topics discussed in this book, I have additional resources listed on this page:

CarmaRecommends.com/**hshpresources**

Here I've listed products, services, and reading recommendations that will help you grow your business with your website.

**66**

*"Gratitude is the fairest blossom which springs from the soul."*

**– Henry Ward Beecher**
American Clergyman and Activist

# Did you enjoy this book?

If you enjoyed this book and received value from it, then I'd like to ask you for a favor: would you be kind enough to leave a review for this book on Amazon? It'd be greatly appreciated! I am thankful for reviews on Goodreads as well.

**66**

*"It is a rare goal that has only one path."*

**– Carma Spence**
Author, Speaker,
Legacy Creation Mentor

# About the Author

Bestselling author of the award-winning book *Public Speaking Super Powers*, Carma Spence is a "geek who speaks."

Although she started college life to become a biologist, she eventually transformed that goal into being a science writer. She earned a Master's degree in Journalism from what *U.S. News & World Report* called the #1 public relations graduate program in the nation.

From there, she worked in marketing and public relations, promoting such organizations as Champagne Deutz, City of Hope National Medical Center, and Blue Shield of California. Involved in marketing—both online and off—for more than 20 years, she is also the author of *57 Secrets for Branding Yourself Online*.

She has won multiple awards for her editorial work and gained exposure for her employers in newspapers such as *The Baltimore Sun* and the *Pasadena Star-News*. During an internship at The Marine Mammal Center, she even got the palm of her hand on the cover of *The Marin Independent Journal!*

Currently, Carma helps entrepreneurs, small business owners, and mid-level executives write, publish, and market their non-fiction books based on the knowledge between their ears even if they've never written before and are crazy busy. She helps her clients unleash what they are uniquely knowledgeable about—their passions, interests, and hobbies (no matter how obscure)— so that they can boldly communicate their message with confidence and create a meaningful and fulfilling legacy. Her superpower is to help people see what is possible for them and guide them on the journey from where they are to where they want to be, vanquishing the Mind Goblins that keep them stuck.

She lives in Minnesota with her husband, cat, and an extensive collection of science fiction books and DVDs.

**66**

*"Be simple and
always take the
next step."*

**– Carl Jung**
Swiss Psychiatrist and Psychotherapist

# Take Your Next Step

Are you ready to write your first or next book?

Are you ready to create a business that leverages authorship, speaking, and coaching?

Do you want to improve people's lives and create an income for you, as well as a legacy for the future?

Carma Spence can help you with your Legacy Creation Hero's Journey so that you can finally write that book you've always wanted to write even if you've never written before and are crazy busy.

To explore whether working with Carma is a good fit for you, set up a no-cost Curious Conversation:

**bookme.name/carmaspence/**
**curious-conversation-with-carma**

**66**

*"Carma has an almost uncanny ability to pick up on what's important and needs focus in a business."*

**– Rev. Rochelle Walden**
Spirit in Business Coach

# Bring Carma Into Your Business or Organization

Carma's authentic, natural style combined with training skills positions her as a top choice for many educational events. She customizes each presentation and training to achieve and exceed the objectives of her clients.

**Contact Carma Today to Begin the Conversation**
**www.carmaspence.com/speaker**